HISTORY OF FUN STUFF

The High Score and Lowdown on Video Games!

D0530345

By Stephen Krensky

Illustrated by Scott Burroughs

Ready-to-Read

Simon Spotlight
New York   London   Toronto   Sydney   New Delhi

SIMON SPOTLIGHT

An imprint of Simon & Schuster Children's Publishing Division

1230 Avenue of the Americas, New York, New York 10020

First Simon Spotlight edition March 2015

Text copyright © 2015 by Simon & Schuster, Inc.

Illustrations copyright © 2015 by Scott Burroughs

All rights reserved, including the right of reproduction in whole or in part in any form.

SIMON SPOTLIGHT, READY-TO-READ, and colophon are registered

trademarks of Simon & Schuster, Inc.

For information about special discounts for bulk purchases, please contact Simon & Schuster Special Sales at 1-866-506-1949 or business@simonandschuster.com.

Manufactured in the United States of America 0215 LAK

2 4 6 8 10 9 7 5 3 1

Library of Congress Cataloging-in-Publication Data

Krensky, Stephen.

The high score and lowdown on video games / by Stephen Krensky ; illustrated by Scott Burroughs.

pages cm. — (History of fun stuff) (Ready-to-read)

1. Video games—Juvenile literature. I. Burroughs, Scott, ill. II. Title.

GV1469.3.K735 2015

794.8—dc23

2014030113

ISBN 978-1-4814-2916-0 (hc)

ISBN 978-1-4814-2915-3 (pbk)

ISBN 978-1-4814-2917-7 (eBook)

CONTENTS

CHAPTER 1
Let the Games Begin

Once upon a time games were played without batteries. Or electricity. There were classic games like chess and checkers, and more recent additions like Monopoly and Clue. Many games involved rolling dice or moving playing pieces around a big board. A limited number of people could play at once. But all that changed once video games exploded onto the scene!

If you want to play video games, you first need a video screen and some kind of controls. The earliest version of this machine to appear had the less-than-fun name of Cathode-Ray Tube Amusement Device. It was patented by Thomas T. Goldsmith Jr. and Estle Ray Mann in 1948.

Players maneuvered a dot on a screen to pass over an object and then pressed a button to "hit" the object. The Cathode-Ray Tube Amusement Device was never released into the marketplace, but it is credited with receiving the first ever patent for an electronic game. Not too shabby!

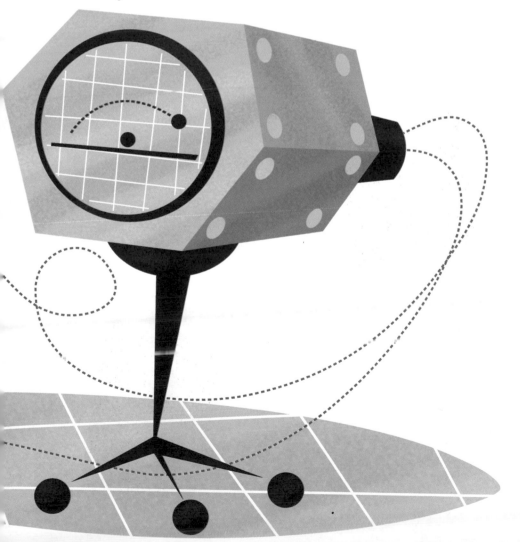

As the 1950s began, nobody thought much about using computers to play games. Computers were used for things like crunching numbers and sorting data. There was a little experimentation, though. A computerized version of tic-tac-toe called OXO was created in 1952, and a few people later programmed computers to play checkers and chess.

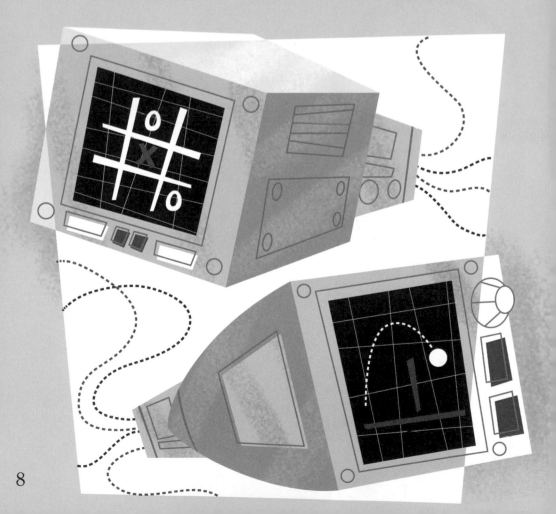

In 1958 a game called Tennis for Two was demonstrated at Brookhaven National Laboratory in New York. Another advance came with Spacewar!, created in 1962. In this game two spaceships on a small screen fired torpedoes at each other. These games were simple, but they were still great achievements for the times.

Then in 1972 Nolan Bushnell, Ted Dabney, and Al Alcorn founded a new game company called Atari. Atari's first release was Pong, a black-and-white arcade game. An electronic "ball" bounced back and forth between two vertical lines that were meant to simulate paddles. Each paddle was controlled by a player. When one player missed the "ball" and it

went off the "court," the other player got a point. If you think this simple kind of electronic Ping-Pong isn't very exciting by today's standards, you're right. But then, in 1975, Atari released a home version of Pong that could be played on an ordinary TV. People were thrilled to have a video game they could actually play at home on their television!

The next step in the evolution of the video game was creating a console that could play more than one game. Believe it or not, the Magnavox Odyssey had done just that in 1972, but it didn't gain popularity as Pong had. In 1977, Atari released a new gaming console, the Atari 2600. Each game came in its own cartridge, which you inserted into the base unit. The games used either joysticks or paddle controllers and were played in color. So now not only could people play video games at home, but they could play them in color, too! The excitement over video games continued to grow.

13

At that time, many video games for consumers focused on moving things around on a TV screen. The game Adventure, created in 1975 by Will Crowther and later enhanced in 1976 by Don Woods, was something different. In this computer game players explored a series of connected caves and confronted fantasy creatures and other obstacles. They moved around by typing simple commands. However, if you tried to do something that was not possible (like use a weapon you didn't possess), the game was quick to make fun of you. This "sense of humor" made the computer seem alive.

CHAPTER 2
Rise of the Arcades

The first mass-market personal computers appeared in 1977. They were too expensive for most people to own. A few games, like Adventure, were available for them, but game makers concentrated on games for the arcades that were springing up in malls and storefronts. Individual arcade games were also very expensive, but the high cost was offset by the fact that people paid a quarter to play each time . . . and many people played the same game for hours on end. Those quarters really added up!

The first big arcade hit was Space Invaders. As the game began, rows of enemy aliens descended from the top of the screen. At the bottom of the screen you controlled a laser cannon that could move to the left or right. From there you fired up at the advancing horde. The player's goal was to get as high a score as possible before getting obliterated by the enemy.

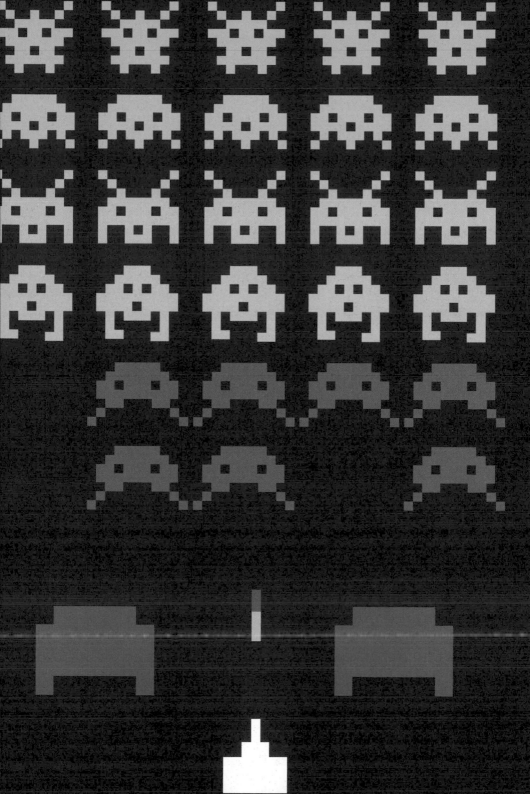

In 1980 Pac-Man became the newest arcade craze. It involved navigating a small round creature through a maze, watching him gobble up little dots along the way while dodging the ghosts that were chasing him. The game was so popular it spurred the creation of Ms. Pac-Man. The next year a Japanese company called Nintendo introduced Donkey Kong, a platform game. Players controlled a character called Jumpman as he raced across levels of a construction site. His goal was to rescue the fair Pauline from a very stubborn gorilla called Donkey Kong. Jumpman was later renamed Mario.

Dozens of other platform games soon appeared, and the video game business was booming.

Everything seemed to be going great for video games—until suddenly it wasn't. Too many home game console systems were now fighting for the public's attention. On a different front, the popularity of the videocassette recorder (VCR) was surging. Taping TV programs at home gave people more options for how to spend their leisure time—giving video

games some serious competition! During this time the market was flooded with some pretty terrible games that had been rushed into production. The result was a backlash against all video games. Between 1983 and 1985 many companies went out of business, devastating the industry.

CHAPTER 3
Home Invasion

Fortunately, like the resilient characters in so many video games, the industry bounced back. In 1985 Nintendo unveiled the Nintendo Entertainment System (NES). It featured a new platform game, Super Mario Bros., which was so well received that it helped to spur sales of the console. Most importantly, though, NES game cartridges now were capable of saving games in progress. This feature forever changed the whole game landscape. It figured prominently in the release of the action-adventure game, The

Legend of Zelda (1987), which centered on the character Link and his quest to rescue Princess Zelda.

In 1989 Nintendo introduced the first major handheld game console, the Game Boy. This new device really shook things up! It was small and portable, yet still big enough to play adapted versions of some existing games. It was also ideal for playing a popular game called Tetris.

Tetris was deceptively simple: A player had to rotate falling blocks of different shapes to create a row across the bottom of the screen. When the row was complete, it would vanish and points would accumulate. There were no characters and no story, but nobody cared. They just played and played and played.

The increased storage capacity in disks called CD-ROMs also spurred improvements. The mysterious puzzle-based adventure, Myst (1993), showcased the beautiful graphics that were now possible. One new format pioneered by id Software was the first-person-shooter game. It debuted

with Wolfenstein 3-D (1992), a World War II adventure, and was soon followed by Doom (1993), which added multi-player support to the first-person perspective. In Doom the player assumed the identity of a space marine sent to investigate a problem on a Martian moon. Intensely action-packed, this game became a runaway bestseller.

By now there were almost too many kinds of games to keep track of (or even to mention here). Sports games from Electronic Arts, like John Madden Football (1988), realistically simulated interactions on various playing fields. The Sim series, beginning with SimCity, allowed you to build your own city and then family and planet. As playing games with other people evolved, you could all play in the same room or in different places through connections over the Internet. But you were still limited to playing with people you had arranged things with ahead of time. That too was about to change. . . .

CHAPTER 4
Conquering the World

While game playing was jumping by leaps and bounds, much of this progress was made possible by new advancements in video game consoles. As the twenty-first century began, the leading video game console was Sony's PlayStation 2. Nintendo's GameCube and Microsoft's Xbox joined it the next year in 2001. New types of games continued to appear, such as Guitar Hero (2005) and Rock Band (2007). They used controllers that worked like real instruments to create musical performances. Inventive controllers were also central to 2006's Nintendo Wii. Its wireless controllers could detect physical motion as well as input from the controller buttons. It encouraged new versions of sports games that could simulate the experience of actually playing the sport.

More powerful consoles and faster Internet speeds signaled the next major shift in gaming. These were the massively multiplayer online role-playing games (MMORPGs). In these games players usually sign on to subscription-based servers, where they enter worlds and interact with players here, there, and everywhere. MMORPGs include well-known brands like Star Wars and Lord of the Rings. World of Warcraft, a fantasy adventure with millions of monthly subscribers, is one especially popular example.

The emergence of the smartphone, heralded by the iPhone in 2007, brought more changes. New and simple games (known as "apps" when they're played on smartphones or tablets) like Angry Birds (2009) and Candy Crush Saga (2012) fascinated the public. These apps were a distinct threat to home-console games.

If people were playing games on their way to school or work, they might be less interested in playing more traditional games when they got home. Plus mobile games cost only a dollar or two, unlike traditional video games, which cost much more. In addition, new games, such as Zynga's Farmville (2009), were widely available for free via social network sites. The game-playing marketplace was changing once again.

By now there's a style of video game for almost everyone. You can play at home on a big screen, at an arcade in a specially outfitted chair, or on a smartphone just about anywhere (except maybe the dinner table!). Games may take minutes, hours, or even months to complete. Some have simple animation, while others have complex graphics that could rival the latest blockbuster movie. You can play a game alone, against the computer, or with players from around the world. The choices may not be unlimited, but they come pretty close.

39

HISTORY
OF FUN STUFF

EXPERT

ON

VIDEO

GAMES

Congratulations! You've come to the end of this book. You are now an official History of Fun Stuff Expert on video games. Feel free to impress your friends and family with all the cool things you've learned. What will come next? Will holographic images or virtual-reality headsets—both of which surround you with the action—be the next frontier? Who knows? Just remember how far video games have evolved over the years. All things considered, what seems impossible now may be closer than you think.

Hey, kids! Now that you're an expert on the history of video games, turn the page to learn even more about video games, plus some geography and math along the way!

The Geography of Japan

Since 1986 Japanese companies like Nintendo and Sony have dominated video games. Sony's PlayStation 2 even holds the record for best-selling video game console! But hot video games aren't all there is to Japan; this country is also home to some *very* hot geographic features, including volcanoes, islands, and hot springs!

Most of Japan's geography is affected by volcanoes. A **volcano** is a piece of land, usually shaped like a mountain, where molten rock, or **magma**, erupts through the ground. More than one hundred active volcanoes are scattered throughout Japan! But why does Japan have so many volcanoes?

It has to do with **tectonic plates**, or chunks of land, which come together like puzzle pieces to form the earth's crust. These plates move slightly over long periods of time, and depending which way they're moving, they can form volcanoes!

SEA OF JAPAN

JAPAN

PACIFIC OCEAN

Underneath the tectonic plates is a layer of magma. When two plates crash into each other, one plate is pushed under while another plate slides up. In between them, magma squeezes through, making its way to the surface.

Japan's most famous volcano is Fujiyama, a **dormant volcano**. A dormant volcano is a volcano that hasn't erupted in a long time, even though there is still ongoing activity inside it.

Living near a place where plates collide can be dangerous: Volcanic eruptions, earthquakes, and tsunamis are more likely to occur! But volcanoes can also create new islands and warm mineral-rich hot springs, and improve the soil to help grow crops.

Remember how volcanoes form? This same action of two plates colliding can also make new islands. Japan consists of four main islands as well as thousands of smaller ones. We call a group of many islands clustered together in the same body of water an **archipelago**.

The Japanese archipelago was formed when one plate sank under another and collided with the superhot layer of magma beneath the earth's crust. Material from the plate melted and then rose to build up the crust, forming volcanoes as well as a series of islands that popped up from the ocean floor.

Japan has become famous for its three thousand plus hot springs, known as *onsen*, most of which are clustered in volcanic belts about the islands.

Many of these hot springs are formed from the heated groundwater near volcanoes, but in other places, water is warmed by layers of hot rock deep within the earth. This second type of spring requires machines to pump the water to the surface. All hot springs have one thing in common, though: They are infused with special minerals that many claim cure aches and illnesses.

Charting the Popularity of Video Games

Businesspeople in the video game industry often use charts and graphs to see how video games are selling and to decide on what types of games they should make.

Line graphs are useful because they show us how something changes over time. It all starts out with a data set, like the one in the chart below.

DATA SET

YEAR	VIDEO GAME SALES (IN BILLIONS)
2002	6.9
2003	7.0
2004	7.3
2005	7.0
2006	7.4
2007	9.5
2008	11.7

We can use this data set to plot points on a grid. By connecting the points, we can make a line graph! A line graph has six major features: the **title, legend, source, y-axis, x-axis,** and **data.**

The **title** explains briefly what a graph is about. The title on our graph is "Video Game Sales," so this graph will show how video game sales have changed over time. The **legend** on the right shows what the line in our line graph represents. The **source** tells others where we found the information to make our graph.

The **y-axis** runs up and down the left side of the graph; it usually tells us the amount of stuff being measured. Here the y-axis represents money in billions of dollars. The **x-axis** runs left to right at the bottom of the graph and generally shows a length of time. In this graph our x-axis is years from 2002 through 2008.

The **data** are points plotted on the graph that represent our data set. We plot points on a graph by tracing up from the year and over from the sales mark. Where the two lines intersect is where our point goes. Once all the points are plotted, we can connect them to make a line.

You can look at the graph to find out how events in video game history affected video game sales. Looking at the huge sales jump in 2007 and 2008, what do you think happened in those years? Flip back to page 36 to find out!

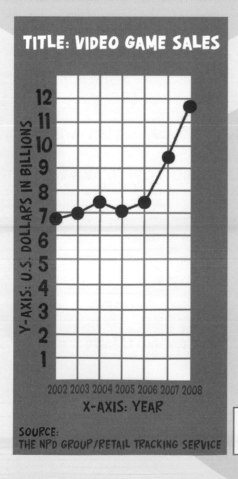

TITLE: VIDEO GAME SALES

Y-AXIS: U.S. DOLLARS IN BILLIONS

12 11 10 9 8 7 6 5 4 3 2 1

2002 2003 2004 2005 2006 2007 2008
X-AXIS: YEAR

SOURCE:
THE NPD GROUP/RETAIL TRACKING SERVICE

LEGEND:
—●— VIDEO GAME SALES

Being an expert on something means you can get an awesome score on a quiz on that subject! Take this

HISTORY OF VIDEO GAMES QUIZ

to see how much you've learned.

1. When was the earliest version of a video game machine patented?

a. 1948   b. 1921   c. 1832

2. In 1972 what company did Nolan Bushnell, Ted Dabney, and Al Alcorn create?

a. Nintendo   b. Atari   c. Sony

3. Pong was a video game version of which famous tabletop game?

a. foosball   b. air hockey   c. Ping-Pong

4. Why were the Atari 2600 and the Magnavox Odyssey different from other game systems before them?

a. They had sound.   b. They could read minds.   c. They could play many different games.

5. Donkey Kong introduced Jumpman, but most people know him better by which name?

a. Zelda   b. Mario   c. Spyro

6. What was one of the reasons for the video game market crash between 1983 and 1985?

a. popularity of VCRs   b. not enough video games to play   c. too few video game consoles

7. In 1986 Nintendo unveiled which gaming system?

a. NES   b. N64   c. Wii

8. Myst, Wolfenstein 3-D, and Doom are all examples of what kind of video game?

a. cartridge   b. CD-ROM   c. cell phone

9. The emergence of what device brought about games such as Angry Birds and Candy Crush Saga?

a. smartphone   b. NES   c. Playstation

Answers: 1.a 2.b 3.c 4.c 5.b 6.a 7.a 8.b 9.a